<u>Depression</u>

A Mind Game

Depression Facts, Diagnosis, Symptoms, Treatment, Causes, Effects, Alternative Medicines, Therapeutic Methods, History, Myths, and More!

By Frederick Earlstein

Copyrights and Trademarks

Disclaimer and Legal Notice

Foreword

Depression is one of the most common mental illnesses in the world; fortunately, it's also one of the most treatable. It is now a common knowledge that it is much easier to get rid of the symptoms of depression when a person hasn't had them for too long. Symptoms that last a long time may, in fact, change the overall structure or functioning of a person's brain. The brain's structure can be changed permanently in ways that aren't desirable. The longer the depression last, the greater the likelihood of having another instance of depression in the future. Perhaps the most negative impact of depression (other than committing suicide) is that it can affect a person's relationship with other people, not just with the family but also with friends, colleagues, and dealing with people in general.

If you think you are depressed or have been showing signs of being in a sad state for a long time, then picking up this book is the first step towards healing! Doing something now can also help reduce the negative impact on the important people in your life, a fair warning though because taking steps to reduce your symptoms will be difficult but hey! Your health and well - being are worth it!

Table of Contents

Introduction:..7

Welcome to the Mind Game 7

Chapter One: Depression and You 11

    Understanding Depression 12

    Myths and Facts 15

    A Brief History of Depression..........................19

Chapter Two: Different Forms of Depression 25

Chapter Three: Causes, Diagnosis, Impacts and Treatments..33

    Causes of Depression 34

    Diagnosis, Sign and Symptoms 37

    Other Symptoms of Depression 41

    Effects of Depression in the Brain 42

    General Trends of Depression among Ethnic or Cultural Groups..44

    Medical Treatments for Depression...............45

    Treatment Phases...51

    Treatment for Post – Partum Depression......53

    Key Elements in Recovering from Depression.............54

    Effects of Untreated Depression 56

Chapter Four: Managing Depression 57

Tips on How to Deal with Depression 58

Avoiding a Relapse Depression.......................................66

What Not to Do When You Are Depress 68

Chapter Five: Holistic Treatments and Therapeutic
Modalities 73

Switch to Nutritious Food and the Right Diet...............74

Holistic Supplements 77

Other Modalities 78

Mind and Body Therapies...79

Chapter Six: How to Help a Depress Person....................85

Tips in Dealing with a Depress Person 86

Chapter Seven: The Future of Depression 97

New Treatments for Depression 98

Deep TMS vs. Surface TMS...101

Promising Treatments for Depression..........................102

Future of Assessing Depression among Patients........105

Bonus Chapter:...109

Index 115

Photo References..119

References 121

Introduction:

Welcome to the Mind Game

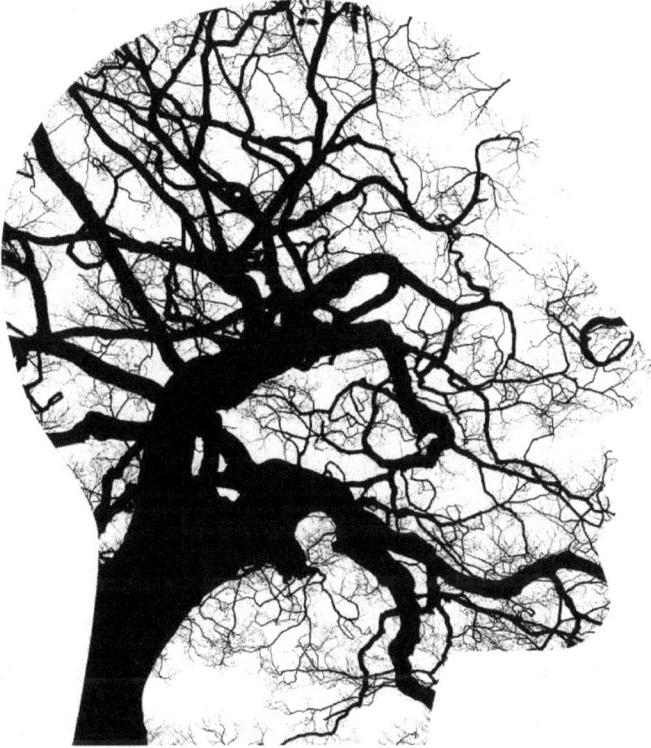

Depression is an inside job killer. And just like many mental illnesses, it could kill a person before he/she even knows it. This is why I call it a mind game. I'm sure you're aware that our brain is the most powerful system this world has ever created because the brain can create things that doesn't even exist, and imagine circumstances even before it happens. The only downside is that it is also perhaps the deadliest weapon that we all share. Deadly not just in terms of having crazy thoughts on how to create wars, murder innocent people or by simply thinking of doing something wrong to others who we wanted to hurt, but also in terms of being deadly for our own selves, for our own being, especially if we undergo through traumatizing experiences or if we let our brain go to dark places. That's where depression sets in, and while there are many factors that trigger the brain or you to get depress, you can always switch it back to normal and happy functioning should you choose to. Yes, it's a choice – depression is indeed a medical condition triggered by many internal and external factors – but at the end of the day it's how you fight your own demons.

The good news is that, it is in fact a mind game, the opponent is yourself (your antagonistic side of the brain) and the player is also you (your protagonist side). You have the power to win if you wanted to but you also have a chance of losing if you let your own brain (the antagonist side) control you and your emotions. So why not give the power to the good side of your brain? Why not do everything you can to defeat your own demons? Of course, it is easier said than done, which is why you need to know your enemy inside out, learn how to defeat depression by learning about it, knowing what triggers it, how it affects you, how you can deal with it and ultimately how you can overcome it. And don't forget to find some allies - your family, peers, medical professionals, or your God.

Equip yourself with knowledge and a supportive team so together you can defeat your own demons. Remember, you don't have to fight your battles alone!

If you want to know more about this condition or help your loved one who is suffering from this quite deadly detriment, then you've chosen the right book! This book contains some of the basic information regarding depression: its scientific facts, history, the myths surrounding it, its different types, the various and subtle symptoms to watch out for, different treatments, diagnosis, and a whole lot more. We will also look at some of the alternative or complementary treatments available, as well as some unconventional recommendations you can try.

Fortunately, in today's world, the knowledge about this common mental issue is evolving – thanks to advancements of science and technology because there are now more ways than ever to combat this problem that has taken so many lives, and in this book we will also share with you the bright future for people who suffer from major depression. Read on!

Chapter One: Depression and You

Depression is a medical condition. It is not just somebody simply feeling sad or down, it is a mental illness in which a person undergoes through a mood that is usually downcast. People who are depressed have lower energy, they are not able to think positively, they don't feel motivated about anything they do even if they enjoyed doing such things before, they don't sleep well and some have problems with their appetite.

This kind of state can happen for many days, weeks, and months which mean that it can be quite sustained especially if the person is not seeking any professional help. Ultimately, a depressed person is not thinking rationally or in ways that they have been thinking before, they're not upbeat, they also feel as if they cannot get up or move around as they usually would (you can probably call it extreme laziness), and sometimes they also entertain thoughts of killing themselves or essentially committing suicide.

Understanding Depression

Depression has been ignored for so long and in some instances, it's not actually regarded as an illness! Even in today's modern world, people who get depress choose to not care about it or not get proper medical treatment because of the social stigma or shame of being diagnosed with a mental disorder. Sometimes depress people also have fears of being put on a medication because it could possibly alter their minds or way of thinking – which is precisely why you needed to go see the doctor in the first place because your mind really needs to be altered and repaired!

nformationternto

When people don't go for treatment even for those who are only experiencing subtle signs, what happens is that more people are developing long – term depression which can ultimately lead to other illnesses like cardiovascular complications – which then develops into having lower immune systems, and they will be more predisposed of other major kinds of conditions, accidents and whatnot.

According to many mental physicians and psychiatrists, depression is certainly the most prevalent mental condition that they mostly encounter and treat. The sad news is that according to the World Health Organization's predictions, depression by the year 2020 will be the leading cause of disability of people not being able to work, and people not being able to be functional in society. And in the long run, this could cost the society as a whole, because of the level of treatment that will be needed. It may also affect the overall quality of performance or production from the labor force.

If a person is not thinking the way he/she ordinarily would, or are thinking so many negative thoughts that it is beginning to crowd out the person's ability to have anything positive come through, that's a major sign of depression. Of course, this kind of symptom is only known by the person itself, it won't be noticeable by other people unless the patient is sharing it to his/her friends. Another major indicators that can be notice by other people is that if a person cannot be cheered up, or if he/she suddenly loss appetite, become lazy to the point that he/she can't even get up on the bed or have a sense of hopelessness, these symptoms are often insidious because it doesn't come up all at once, it all starts slowly until it gets in the person's head.

Once depressed people acquire and prolong these conditions, they will eventually wear down mentally, and they're ability to cope with the everyday ordinary stresses is lessened or diminished and so they may not be functional as they use to be in their social life, and at work. If you or your loved one is showing signs of prolonged sadness or low – energy state or even subtle changes in the mood or behavior, you should seek medical help or just even tell a close friend or loved one about it.

Usually medical professionals conduct a general interview with the patient, their families, their friends or close loved one so that they can know the person's family or genetic history (if in case, depression runs in the family), as well as the patient's medical history (if they had taken any illegal drugs, had any previous problems that can be related to depression, or if there was an incident in their life that triggered their brain to experience depression). After which, doctors will conduct a mental status exam where they seat and ask targeted questions that are designed to help the evaluator – either the psychiatrist or therapist etc. – to see how the brain is working so that they can get the sense of what the patient's mood is like, how the patient responds to certain questions, and generally how the brain works during this depressive state. Once the doctors finish conducting the personal history of the patient, the mental status exam, and have done some discussions with their loved ones they can then diagnose what type of depression the patient has as well as determine how mild or severe the condition is.

This way it will let your good side of the brain know that you are not in this battle alone, that people can and will help you so that you can overcome this illness.

Myths and Facts

In this section, you will learn the most common myths surrounding depression so that it can provide some enlightenment for you and help you manage your condition more or that of your loved one.

Myth #1: Mood swings particularly for teens or adolescents are normal and are part of growing up

That is not entirely true, yes mood swings are part of growing up but if you are a teenager and you are consistently changing moods for no reason, it can actually be an indicator that you are suffering with depression. This psychological condition actually affects people of all ages, so if you experience mood swings that are frequent and often quite extreme, seek professional help immediately.

Myth #2: If you think your friend is undergoing depression, then he/she is responsible to ask help or share their feelings and not you because it will come across as betrayal of trust or you might look stupid

First of all, if you are a real friend, you should by all means make sure that your friend is okay. You should care for them, even if he/she is not sharing anything with you. Other than that, depression will not just drain your friend but also you (physically and emotionally) and could possibly distort your way of thinking somehow. So if you notice that your friend is showing signs of depression, try to make him/her share something with you, because it can actually save their life. Help him/her win this battle and seek help from family members or doctors as soon as possible. Making promises of not telling anyone is good but you have to also keep in mind that if things get out of control, your friend's life should be your top priority. Sharing something with your friend's family member is also a good thing so that they will be able to notice signs if any, and act on it.

Myth #3: Sharing your depression or talking about it will only make your condition worse

This is what I've been pointing out early on, if you don't talk to anyone about it and only "fight your battles" alone you will certainly end up being more depress, and worse nobody will be there for you when you go through tough times – and you will. Talk to a counselor, a psychiatrist, your parents, your close friend or a social worker so that they can help you process your feelings, your thoughts and be able to help out with your issues and at least provide support so that you can reduce the symptoms.

Myth #4: If you are depress, you are weak

Depression is indeed a serious psychological disorder, but it doesn't mean that you are crazy, weak or even abnormal; it just means that you are suffering from something that is affecting the quality of your life and that of others, just like cancer or any other illnesses. If your fear prevents you from reaching out to people because you think that they will regard you as weak or someone who is "crazy," you'll never find true happiness and peace because you just proved them right. Everyone in this world go through depression at some point in their lives, it's something we all share – just like a sin. It's part of being human, so turn this "weakness" to a strength by seeking professional help and conquer your fears by working towards making yourself better so you can win this deadly game in your mind. Remember, courage is only found in fear.

Myth #5: Depression is just a form of sadness or "blues," it will eventually go away

Sometimes even if you will it, depression does not just go away, it's a process and it will take some time before you actually recover from its symptoms. This condition consists of very persistent hopelessness and helplessness, and the reason why many depress people commit suicide is because they feel as if they are totally worthless, this feelings and thoughts last for a long time if not treated properly.

Myth #6: You will be put on medications forever if you seek medical treatment

While it may be true, most psychiatrists say that there are a lot of many depress people who completely recover from this condition especially if they seek help before it even gets worse. They'll be able to help you get to the root of the problem, work through your issues, and complete the therapy which means that you will eventually wean off the medications. The amount of medications as well as the period of time you take them will greatly depend on the severity of your condition or how well you adjust with it. Many people treated with depression are not necessarily drinking meds for the rest of their life; it's all a matter of completing your treatment to slowly but surely recover from your depression.

A Brief History of Depression

Ancient Greece and Rome

Depression is known as "melancholia" during the time of Ancient Greece around 400 B.C. There were many depictions and portraits that exhibit the telltale symptoms of melancholy or depression like lack of motivation to eat and bathe, frequent crying, fatigue, excessive sleeping, and feelings of worthlessness. Back then, if a person is "gloomy" or downtrodden what they do is conduct a purification ceremony to get rid of "avenging spirits" that causes such gloomy effect on a person.

During Hippocrates' time around the 4th century, melancholia is classified as a mental illness. Ancient physicians including Hippocrates believed that this depressive state is caused by the imbalance of bodily fluids because back then scientists and physicist claims that there are four substances in the body, they are blood, black and yellow bile, and phlegm. And if a person has a disease it was the result of a lack or excess of one of these body fluids so these ancient doctors way of curing depression or melancholy is via bloodletting, medications or purging to bring the "balance" back to these fluids. Other Greek philosophers believed that slight melancholic temperament is actually a sign of genius. Philosophers like Aristotle, Ajax, Socrates, and Plato had symptoms of depression, and it was this gloomy mood that allowed them to become creative and do great things.

Ancient Roman physicians and philosophers like Galen also believed that melancholia is related in having an

imbalance in the blood but he got one thing right when he theorized that some people are born with this kind of temperament – which is what we call now as genetic influences or family history – wherein these patients make the predispose and prone
to the condition.

In the next 400 years, the Greeks and Romans competed and debated about the causes and possible treatments for this mental illness. They had several philosophical as well as spiritual theories and many remedies was brought about to cure this "spiritual or mental disease" like the use of potions, purification ceremonies, philosophical reflections, drinking certain food products and the likes.

Medieval Ages

During the Middle Ages, the classic spiritual idea and approach of being rooted in one's disfavor or punishment from the Gods, only this time it was the God of Christianity. Many priests and clerics believe that having melancholy is a sign that a person is being possess by demons, and that whoever suffers from it must be living sinfully which is why they must repent or do hard labor as punishment so that God will forgive them. A book written during the medieval times called "The Noonday Demon" associates sin with melancholy, have somehow given rise to the social stigma that carried on and surrounds depression in the modern era.

Renaissance Era

Philosophers and thinkers during the Renaissance era have perhaps the best take when it comes to melancholy. During this time they view the illness not as a sign of punishment from God or a sin but as a catalyst of genius and greatness. Many aristocrats, philosophers and writers during this time actually regarded themselves as having a touch of melancholy which made it somewhat "fashionable." According to many Renaissance philosophers, melancholic are individuals who strive to understand the mystery of this world and the glory of God, but since human knowledge is limited and will never fully understand the wholeness of life, these people was left in a state of despair and gloominess. Melancholy became a thing that people took great pride in during the Renaissance. Such intellectual complexities and soulfulness gave birth to many literary masterpieces including plays that have gloomy and downcast themes including Shakespeare's Hamlet.

Age of Enlightenment and the Romantic Era

Science and technology is beginning to advance human's knowledge when it comes to finding the possible causes and treatments for many illnesses. During the age of enlightenment, melancholy was regarded as a malfunction of the human brain, and that it affects nerves in the brain due to many external factors like lack of labor. The best remedy perhaps is to focus on doing something significant every day or keeping oneself busy just like the labor that people do in rural areas because such activities produce people who are emotionally robust unlike those who are living in cities where everything is relax therefore making them vulnerable to depression.

The theory was turned again during the Romantic period because during this time they revived the idea of having gloomy moods as a sign of genius just like in the Renaissance era. They call it the "Age of Introversion," and they celebrated the idea of intuition and emotion that aren't only found in joy but also in sorrow. It was perhaps a purposeful sadness which brought about many dark, gloomy, and sad writings of poetry, and other literature. The illness was a way to discover one's self and being connected with one's soul.

20th Century to Present Day

The advancement of psychology and medical technologies paved the way for physicians and scientists to better understand melancholy and how it affects the human mind. During this time, famous psychologist Sigmund Freud popularized psychoanalysis techniques in an attempt to alleviate and cure this illness. The illness was eventually treated as a mental disorder brought about by many factors and not something related to the spirit or other philosophical theories without a scientific basis. Around this time, another psychologist named Adolf Meyer proposed that the term for such mental illness should be depression since it is a prolonged condition, and not just something that can be treated once.

As the field of medicine progresses, many psychiatrist and physicians discovered various trigger factors of depression and how it plays a role under the umbrella of various mental illnesses. Many medicines were manufactured to alleviate the symptoms like antidepressants, and many therapeutic as well as psychological techniques were also develop to help depress patients cope up with their mental disorder.

Chapter Two: Different Forms of Depression

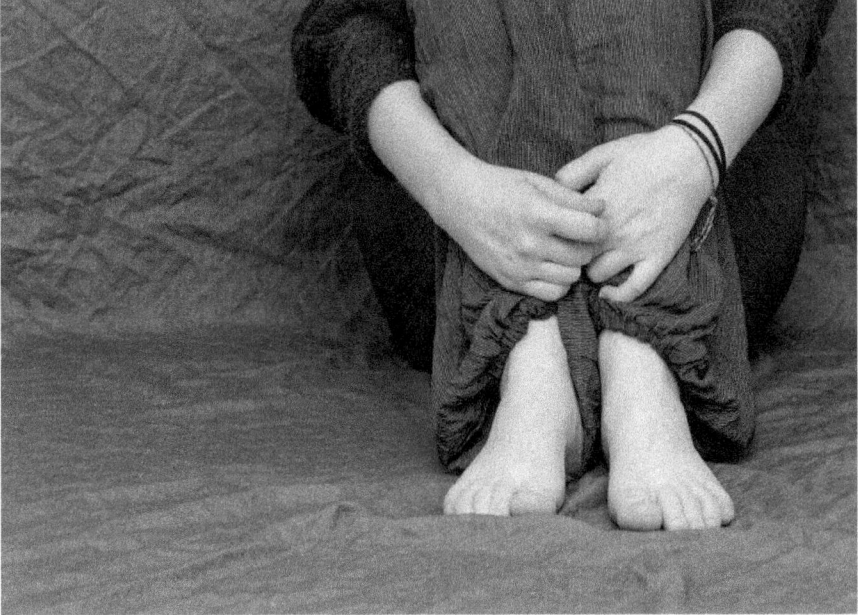

6 out of 10 people are usually diagnosed with depression; it has become a major problem not just in United States but also in other countries. Most of the people affected are either adolescents or young professional adults, and although this mental disorder affects any age, they are also the ones who are prone to committing suicide or are most likely inclined to become depress for various reasons. There are several types of depression, and they ranged in severity.

In this section you'll be given an overview about the many types of depression as well as its common signs and distinction.

Major Depression

Major depression is the most common type of depression with 7% of U.S. population having this at any given time. It lasts two weeks and some people only experience one episode of it

Signs of Major Depression:

- Extreme sadness
- Hopelessness
- Lack of sleep
- Lack of eating
- Suicidal attempts

Dysthymia

About two percent of population in United States has dysthymia. This type of depression is different than the other forms because it is more chronic, and long – term depression lasting for 6 months to more than a year.

Signs of this type are very similar to major depression but it is less severe.

Post - Partum Depression

This type of depression is not actually a popular one and is not really talked about because it is something that is related after a woman gave birth. It's also something that new moms don't talk about because of course, when you give birth to a baby; you're supposed to feel happy and excited about it not the other way around but unfortunately for some people that's not the case. It's very common for new moms to have some sort of sadness; in fact 85% of moms experience this feeling after giving birth. However, for some women they experience a more intense sadness which could lead to depression. They could experience it for a few weeks or even a few months after giving birth.

Signs of Post - Partum Depression
- Most new moms gain weight
- They don't feel a connection to their infant
- They fear that they are going to hurt their baby
- They think that they're not going to be a good mother

Seasonal Affective Disorder (SAD)

This type of depression only happens during a certain season which is usually winter. When it starts getting gloomy, dark or cold outside, some people tend to experience depression. There are about 4 to 6 percent of Americans who experience seasonal affective disorder, but it usually occurs only for a few months within a year.

Signs of Seasonal Affective Disorder:
- Anxiety
- Irritability
- Weight gain
- Other common depressive symptoms

Atypical Depression

According to most psychologists, atypical depressions are not usually understood and it is much underdiagnosed.

Signs of Atypical Depression:
- Heavy feeling on the limbs or legs
- Oversleeping
- Overeating
- Relationship problems

Psychotic Depression

Psychosis is a mental state that is categorized by a false belief or delusion as well as false sights or sounds otherwise known as hallucinations. According to mental health organizations, 20% of people who gets depress can eventually be so severe that they start seeing, hearing or feeling things that are not there.

Signs of Psychotic Depression:
- People suffering with psychotic depression oftentimes aren't able to speak or don't want to speak
- Extreme laziness
- Suffering from hallucinations

Bipolar Disorder

This mental disorder is associated with depression and it is actually treated as a form of mental illness on its own but it can also be considered under the umbrella of depression. Bipolar disorder is a condition wherein the person experiences high moods (mania) and low moods (depression). Hypomania is when a person experiences a lot of energy but has poor judgment that suddenly changes to low moods or a depressive state within a short period of time. The symptoms can go back and forth and within multiple times in a year.

Situational Depression

Otherwise known as "adjustment disorder," this type of depression is usually triggered by a stressful event in a person's life like a death in the family, traumatic experience, loss of a job or dream and even a bad breakup in a person's relationship. This is a very common type of depression but fortunately it doesn't last for a long time. It only lasts for a week up to a few months but it can turn into major depression if a person don't get proper treatment or doesn't have anyone to talk to or share their problems.

Pre – Menstrual Dysphoric Disorder (PMDD)

This is actually a new form of depression, and in fact one that is very controversial because a lot of people think about it as PMS (Pre – menstrual syndrome), but some people say otherwise while others think that it shouldn't be classified as a form of depression. PMDD is a pre – menstrual symptom that usually happens two weeks before a woman begins their menstrual cycle. With PMS symptoms include mood swings, a woman's boobs hurt or even crave things but with PMDD it's actually those symptoms but much more severe. Some people who have PMDD can actually become suicidal just two weeks before their menstruation which is why it can also be very serious, and if you are experiencing it in any way, it's better to at least ask a doctor about it to make sure it's not some sign of depression and be able to prevent it before it gets worse.

Chapter Three: Causes, Diagnosis, Impacts and Treatments

Knowing the causes, symptoms, effects and treatments for depression is key to managing it and recovering from this mental illness. If you left depression untreated, it can actually cause other mental problems or even chronic health issues. Early detection is essential when it comes to preventing depression, the symptoms may be subtle and something that is usually being ignored but over time if these symptoms are not properly address can lead to the development of depression.

In this chapter, you'll learn a lot about the causes of depression, it's short and long term impacts, criteria for diagnosis as well as medical treatments usually prescribed by the doctors. You'll also learn some key elements in recovery and also the common groups of people who are more prone to depression.

Causes of Depression

Depression is caused by many factors including genetic factors, social factors, psychological factors and personal factors. All these stressors come into play which means that if you want to prevent depression or being in a low – state or negative state of mind for a long period of time, the best course of action to take is to educate oneself as to the kinds of things that contribute to the buildup of depression.

Common situations that causes depression in people nowadays includes loss of a job or being unemployed, where a person is unable to provide for a family or if a person feel as if he/she doesn't have a "purpose" in life can lead to negative thinking which will then lead to being depress; another example is if a person has been diagnosed with a serious or terminal illness can also lead to depression – the financial burden, the family being worried, the thought of you're not going to have a normal life anymore or that you don't have that much time left – this personal and psychological factors can trigger a person's depressive state including the death of a beloved. Perhaps, the most common factor that causes major sadness or leads to long term depression is a breakup, a divorce or some sort of separation from a loved one. Broken relationships will not just break someone's heart or cause damage to one's emotional being, most of the time it also messes up their brain, and put's a person in a state of negative emotion.

Another external factor could be traumatizing events such as abuse, accidents, or other life – threatening occurrences. If a person undergoes a shocking or fearful situation, it can lead to a psychotic effect and if it is not process or treated properly with the help from a professional it can develop long – term depression or other mental disorders.

Bad diet, chronic fatigue, and anxiety can also be a factor when it comes to developing depression which is why it's important to keep one's health in check, not just mental and emotional health but the physical health as well because it all contributes to the possible buildup of depression and other serious illnesses. A strong body will have a strong mind; a person is most likely to overcome depressive symptoms and stop it from further development if he/she is taking care of his/her well – being.

Part of the ways that could work in preventing such causes is to understand that you are always at risk in facing one of these stressors or triggers and in line with that, you should be able to identify or notice this subtle signs or get ahead of these negative or unforeseen circumstances by protecting yourself or doing something once this trigger factors happen. The ways you can do to help you not develop depression is through regular exercise, being involve in religious organizations or being a member of social clubs, and having a certain hobby. Following the doctor's medication or going for a counsel as soon as you think such factors are already causing you to get upset is very crucial because you are stopping it from getting worse.

For those who have a more genetic or biologically driven type of depression that may have run in the family, you may be in need of medication or a physical regimen since it's more of a biological factor – something that runs in your blood and something you can't really control. Sometimes it's also the cause of hormonal imbalance in the body that triggers the brain to be depressed.

Antiviral drugs taken for long periods of time can also cause or increase the risk of having depression.

Diagnosis, Sign and Symptoms

As with all diagnosis or exhibit a certain number of factors or signs to qualify for the diagnosis – in this case the depressive symptoms but it should be for a period of time so that other situational factors or fleeting sadness can be filtered out. When it comes to depression in general, there are 9 potential symptoms a person can exhibit, and in order to receive a depressive diagnosis, a patient should possess or show at least five symptoms that will be discuss in this section.

Vegetative Symptoms – these symptoms are indicative for deterioration in a physical activity or physical components of depression.

- **Irritability or depress mood all day** – the way to tell the difference between being a normal person just having a bad or moody day from symptoms of depression is that if this kind of mood lasts for more than a week or so. Showing one or two signs of being in a sad state could be alarming and should be monitored because that could actually start the whole depressive state but it has to last in a consistent or perhaps frequent basis and not just momentarily.

- **Lack of Pleasure or Loss of Interest -** not receiving pleasure in most things or not being interested anymore in things that you normally like to do before could be a signal of being depress. The loss of pleasure or loss of capacity to experience pleasure is something you should watch out for especially if there's no replacement – for example if you like playing basketball before and then suddenly you stop doing that but you haven't replace it with another hobby or sport, and you also begin interest in trying out things or doing things you normally have fun doing is a major sign that depression is building up.

- **Change in Appetite or Significant Weight Loss/Gain** – If you are a regular eater or say fond of eating and then all of a sudden you lose appetite that could be a sign that you are depress. If there's a shift from normal functioning in your eating habits that should be taken into consideration. If for example you are a picky eater ever since, that cannot be considered a sign of depression. But if you are a healthy eater then suddenly became a picky eater over the course of a few weeks that maybe a sign that you're depress.

- **Sleeping Habits** – If your sleeping habits changes either sleeping more or less than you normally would could again be a sign of depression. You're looking for a change that is quite different from a previous state. For example, if you tend to have a good night sleep but then you can no longer sleep well at night or if you only sleep for a regular 8 hours but now you want to sleep longer than that and you maintain that kind of sleeping pattern for a long time that's a symptom.

- **The energy level changes** – depress people just don't want to get out of bed or up off the couch and may linger for a long time without doing much. They may also report fatigue even if they're not doing anything hard.

- **Agitation or Lethargic** – depress people may tend to feel agitated or being highly intense, sometimes its opposite which is feeling lethargic or kind of having a slow feeling or fatigue along with a decrease in energy level.

- **Feeling Worthless or Excessively Guilty** – Worthless in a way that that there's no sense of living or that they don't have a purpose in life. And guilty in a way of feeling bad about the choices, decisions or even one's beliefs. Self – esteem also decreases.

- **Indecisiveness** – If you are having difficulty thinking or concentrating for no reason, then that could be a sign that you're depress. Not being able to focus in something don't necessarily mean that a person is depress or has a mental disorder, but if such things occur on a regular basis and it's not something that is being experienced before that could be another factor for being diagnose with depression.

- **Morbid or Suicidal Thoughts** – If you are being preoccupied lately with suicidal thoughts or thinking about death that could mean you are depress. If you notice yourself watching films with a depressive theme or listening to sad music, and you don't do that before that could be a sign but it doesn't also mean that you are depress or you will become depress although it might be something to watch out for. Depress people are more likely to gravitate towards morbid themes in music, movies or even art.

These symptoms should be exhibited for at least two weeks or fourteen days in a row because it will help filter out temporary feelings of sadness or situational issues from something that is more serious or based on biological factors.

Other Symptoms of Depression

Aside from the symptoms mentioned above, there are also other factors that need to be taken into consideration before being diagnose with depression. This includes if a person is reporting a significant feeling of distress or impairment in the body's functioning. Or they're not producing or tending to the things as well as they are used to.

Withdrawal and Isolation

You should also be able to monitor any signs of isolation or withdrawal from the world. If you or someone you know is spending more time alone that could be another sign.

Body language

Body language is another giveaway such as poor eye contact. Depress people carry themselves in a certain way and their body language gives that feeling of depression.

Grievances or Bereavement

Unresolved grief could be another symptom especially if the person loss something or someone important, because for some people it will be hard to process. Grief is already a major depressive factor but when someone get stuck that could be evolve in serious depression.

Hopelessness

If the person feels like there's no hope or there's "no light at the end of the tunnel" or there's simply no way out of a situation, it will make the person possess a negative state of mind or become moody.

Effects of Depression in the Brain

When people are depressed their thinking ability is somehow changed. Depress people just can't think as clearly because there's a lot of stuff that's going on in their head all at once. During those depressive periods, they will certainly have cognitive impairment; brain chemistry is different which means that neurotransmitters in the brain are not functioning in the same way they should function. This is the reason why one of the solutions to depression is medication.

Depression as mentioned earlier is episodic which means that there's a potential to have a relapse or remitting depression. So if a person had a depressive episode, he/she is more likely to have other depressive episodes in the future. And just like any other serious illness like diabetes or epilepsy or whatnot, a person can also suffer from chronic depression that goes away and then comes back eventually. When people are treated and the depressive symptoms, as mentioned in the previous section, are resolved the brain chemistry changes and that is a good thing. Sometimes when people are very depress it affects their overall performance in work, school or other day to day activities, they could turn into drugs and alcohol, junk food or other forms of bad behavior.

Medications for depression don't change a person's brain for life but it changes the brain while the meds are being taken. The problem is that when you just use medication, and you don't learn other forms of treatment like therapy or other psychological coping strategies, if you're not on medication anymore how will you deal or manage the depression? It doesn't permanently change the brain but there's always a short term and long term effects that is both good and bad.

Medications don't create long term problems but it also does not create long term solutions, it just solves the problem while you use it at a certain period. This is why part of the effective treatment for depression is aside from the help of medicines, the patient should also learn new skills, behaviors, ways of thinking or coping strategies that a patient can carry over time even if there's no medicine intake.

General Trends of Depression among Ethnic or Cultural Groups

There are indeed people from certain cultures who tend to experience more types of mental illness like depression than others including the African – American community, Caucasians and even Latinos. These cultures might have a pre – disposition towards developing depression based on a variety of factors. However, most psychologists agree that the danger about these studies is that it may set up another type of social stigma or another kind of issue which will make more depress people shy away from getting proper treatment.

We have to understand the general trend in terms of who gets depression or the kind of people who are more prone to being depressed like a certain race, ethnic background, history or whatnot, and also take into consideration a certain individual's experience that may not fit that trend.

There has been a trend in suicidal behaviors when it comes to young African – Americans males, and Latino females who underwent teenage pregnancies are also predispose to developing depression. A trend in senior citizens living in nursing homes and tends to be away from their families are also generally dispose to depression. These kinds of trends are what most psychologists encounter.

Medical Treatments for Depression

The objectives in treating depression includes the reduction of the signs and symptoms, restoration of normal psychological functioning, and complete resolution of the disorder to prevent the likelihood of recurrence or relapse depression. Initially, there are certain factors that are being considered by the physician before giving any kind of treatment to the depressive patient; this includes the understanding the severity of the case, the impact of the different stressors (both internal and external), other health conditions, the preferred treatment of the patient as well as the insurance coverage.

Once these factors are determined, the attending physician or psychologist will then conduct necessary diagnosis to further learn about the patient's condition or to determine the type of depression this patient has, this is done through checking the mental status of the patient through psychological tests, interviewing the patient as well as his/her family and friends, and overall health examination to see if there's any underlying causes or triggers that paved the way in developing depression.

Motivational Interviewing

This is the initial type of treatment given to patients; doctors are most likely to recommend the patient to increase their activities or productivity to improve the condition or at least alleviate the depressive symptoms.

Recommended activities may include:

- Exercise at least 3 times or more in a week for about 30 minutes or more
- Recommendation of more nutritious food
- Become engage in social or enjoyable activities
- Do relaxation techniques
- Sleep for at least 8 hours a day at a certain period of time.

Pyschotherapy

Another form of treatment usually given for patients diagnosed with mild to moderate depression is psychotherapy. It can either be interpersonal or cognitive behavioral, and can also be performed individually or with a group. Sometimes, an antidepressant will be needed alongside psychotherapy treatment if the patient has severe sleeping problems like insomnia, anxiety, other mental disorders and suicidal thoughts (anhedonia). However, psychotherapy is not an effective treatment for people who have seer cases of depression or relapse depression as well as severe psychotic depressive disorders. Some patients could also decline this treatment provided that they have been treated with medication before or if they prefer only being treated with a medication.

Medications

Medication is essentially given to all patients diagnosed with any forms of depression but it should be aided with therapy or counseling that will provide as the support system of the patient so that he/she will recover faster. Meds alongside proper therapy works best because it will instill he patient some new behaviors, optimism, and a better mindset. Clinical management is very important if the patient is being given medication especially to those people who have very depressive symptoms like isolation, withdrawal, pessimism, low energy or suicidal attempts; otherwise it could worsen the condition and could make the patient drug dependent.

A patient should be closely monitored if he/she was given antidepressants to prevent the symptoms from worsening; sometimes it could make the patient more suicidal, and may have fluctuations in their behavior especially if the dosage or times of intake is changed.

There's a certain criteria that should be taken into consideration before physicians recommend a certain medication to a depress patient this includes the following:

- Prior response to antidepressants or other medications (for patients who previously took any medication)
- Concurrent medications
- Other health issues (if any)
- History of the patient's relatives and their responses to certain medications

Some guidelines for patients when it comes to taking medications:

- Only take the prescribed medication; do not self – medicate or try other antidepressants
- Antidepressants should be taken for 14 to 28 days every day to notice the effects
- Learn about the side effects or consult with your doctor on how to resolve those side effects if any
- If a medication is stopped before six months, there's a chance of relapse, some antidepressants may also cause withdrawal symptoms if not properly taken.
- Make sure to continue taking in the medication even if you're feeling better, and follow the doctor's advice regarding how long it should be taken.

- Make sure to keep up with your counseling or therapy to ensure that you are responding well with medication
- Meds will not change your brain structure or even your personality; it actually helps in restoring neuro - patterns so that you can go back to normal functioning.
- Never drink alcohol or any other harmful substance with medication

Light Therapy

Light therapy is used for patients who only have seasonal depression. It is a light box device that is usually being given as treatments to patients especially during the "dark or gloomy" months like from September to March. Most of the time patients are advised to do 10,000 lux every day for 30 minutes.

Electroconvulsive Therapy (ECT)

This treatment is given for patients with severe forms of depression or a condition that is often accompanied with loss of appetite, suicidal attempts or psychotic behaviors. This could be a treatment option if meds or other types of counseling therapies were not effective but a full assessment by the psychologist should be done.

Treatment Phases

Acute Treatment - this is done for the first 12 weeks for patients who are currently experiencing severe depressive symptoms or even those who have mild to moderate symptoms (for prevention).

- Patients should be seen at least 3 times by the psychiatrist/psychologist for the first 12 weeks
- Psychologists often recommend the patient to give them a call if in case they experience any unexpected medication reactions
- Patients who will exhibit more severe symptoms are referred to behavioral health.
- Patients who have severe depressive symptoms on medication with sudden onset should be closely observed and may need to see the doctor more often.

- Once depressive symptoms are resolve, the patient can make an appointment every 4 to 12 weeks.

Doctors usually assessed the patient within 4 to 6 weeks after depressive symptoms are resolved to check if he/she is responding well to the drug therapy, within the next 6 to 12 weeks assessment for psychotherapy is being done.

If patients are not responding within 6 weeks that the medication is given or have only partially respond within 12 weeks, other treatment options are given like the following:

- Medical assessment
- Change in medication
- Second medication
- Behavioral health recommendation
- Referral to a professional psychotherapist

Continuation Therapy - this is for the purpose of avoiding or preventing relapse depression or recurrence. This is usually done for the next 4 to 9 months.

- The patients are advised to continue the medication for the next 4 to 9 months after depressive symptoms are gone.
- If the patient has no signs of symptoms for 4 to 9 months after a depressive episode, then recovery could be declared and treatment could be stop.

Maintenance Therapy – this is for the purpose of preventing new depressive episodes, most of the time patients are advised to have a long – term maintenance therapy if he/she had more than 3 episodes because it has greater chances of relapse. This is usually done for 1 year to a lifetime visit.

Treatment for Post – Partum Depression

When it comes to post – partum depression (depression occurring among moms after giving birth), the first order of treatment is usually psychotherapy because it has been proven to be an effective treatment, and can be done individually or with a group. It is also not risky compared to being given with medication since it can affect breastfeeding.

If medication is prescribed for women who are breastfeeding, the usual medications are Sertraline or

Paroxetine because so far it doesn't have any side effects to the infants who are being nursed or breastfed.

Women who have severe post – partum depression may need a different approach in treatment like pharmacotherapy, crisis intervention, social support groups or may be referred to psychiatric care because it can evolve to major depression.

Key Elements in Recovering from Depression

Early and continued treatment as well as understanding that depression has remissions or relapse components are key elements in recovering from depression and also preventing another serious depressive episodes from happening. Sustained treatment is needed especially for people who have just passed the phase of medication intake, a patient should not stop being engaged in behavioral treatments or counseling/therapies because it necessary for continued healing since depressive episodes can recur. Recovery does not only depend on medication or even continued therapy, it also depends on what happens in the patient's social or personal life.

Psychologists/therapists also make sure that their patients are socially connected to friends, family or other social environment in which the person is existing like religious affiliations, organizations, clubs or whatnot, something that also helps perpetuate wellness on the outside.

Wellness in terms of mental health is not only about being given a medication or counseling, it's actually about feeling balance and functional in a patient's social or personal environment. One has to really be educated and take mental health seriously because people nowadays are only focusing so much on the physical aspect of the body like getting that abs, being in shape, measuring the number of steps etc., while this is also important most of us don't actually consider caring for our mental and emotional aspect which is often why people gets easily depress if something like a terrible event, stressful factors or unforeseen circumstances happens.

Early detection is very crucial so that the patient can be given treatment as soon as possible and be able to reduce or manage the depressive symptoms because if not, this small depressive episodes can lead to serious depression, loss of a job, other medical illnesses, broken relationships, bad vices, destructive behaviors all the way to suicide. Getting involved with depression early on, even with the smallest form of symptoms or negativity is very important because it can actually save a life.

Effects of Untreated Depression

Here are some of the effects if you left depression untreated:

- Tardiness or lots of missed work days
- Refraining from working
- Decrease in productivity
- Fatigue
- Psycho and Emotional disturbances
- Loss of concentration
- Chronic Health Issues

Chapter Four: Managing Depression

Many people think that depression is a mental disorder that can be cured – well, the answer to that not entirely because it's actually an on – going process. It's not like getting a cold where if you just take a rest or drink the meds you'll eventually be cured of it completely. Depression is similar to stress, it's something that cannot be entirely cured but it can definitely be managed. Being depress happens to anyone, so it's perfectly fine that you are depress but it's also important to note that it is something you can handle. Whatever you're feeling right now can be changed.

In this chapter, we'll you some guidelines on how you can manage depression, what you can do once you notice triggering factors like stress, and the things you should not do when you are depress.

Tips on How to Deal with Depression

- **An Exercise a Day Can Make Depression Go Away!**

You probably know already the importance and benefits of exercise (as if it's not being emphasized enough when it comes to health related issues) not just for mental disorders but in a person's general health. When it comes to dealing with depression, exercise can help because it releases body chemical called endorphins. Endorphins are also known as the "feel good" hormone, and once you exercise; your body is going to release these chemicals and will help in making you feel better.

So whenever you are feeling sad or low, just try to do a bit of exercise and think back to how you felt whenever you accomplish even a simple routine or complete a session. The trick for you to get your body moving is to not set a goal too high; don't promise yourself in committing say an hour of exercise or that you'll complete one full session because if you don't chances are, it will trigger you to feel like a failure thus making you go back in a depressive state. What you can do is to take small actions everyday like committing to jog in place for 5 to 10 minutes or say running outside for just 15 minutes or even just doing 10 pushups a day. Accomplishing something will make you feel good, and dong a simple exercise everyday can surely activate those endorphins.

- **Freshen Up!**

Taking a bath can surely make you feel great, but there's actually a better way of doing it! Don't just take showers, take *cold* showers! What you can do is to take a shower as you normally would with lukewarm water or hot water, soap up or put a shampoo, then instead of rinsing off with the lukewarm water, rinse it off with cold shower! It will be quite shocking for your body at first, but it will eventually get used to it. It's something like doing the "ice bucket challenge." Taking cold showers is going to change your state or your mood, and will dramatically make your body feel good.

- **Feed Your Body Right and the Mind will follow!**

The logic behind eating nutritious food is simple, think of your body as a machine, a luxury car perhaps, if you own a Rolls Royce or a Lamborghini will you put cheap gas in it? Will you "feed" the car with oil that will damage its system? Of course not! Same way with our body and your mind! If you eat the right foods (that means no junk, less sodas and less sweets etc.) like vegetables and fruits on a consistent basis it can certainly boost your mood. So if you're eating too much process foods, too much sugar or caffeine, and too many bad foods just slowly cut it down or get into a diet because these bad eating habits will surely affect your body and mind which will then contribute to having low energy or triggering your depressive state.

- **Speak Up!**

It's very hard for people undergoing depression to speak up especially for men. In fact, many psychologists believe that this is the main reason why many commit suicide, and why there are probably more men who have higher suicidal cases than women. Men are mostly afraid to open up or afraid to talk to someone unlike most women.

Speaking up or communicating your feelings with someone is the biggest step you can take to manage your depression. Showing your emotion is not a weakness, it's in fact a sign of strength and courage because you are at least trying to share your feelings to someone even if it's hard or even if you're scared. Once you open up to someone, you're going to feel a weight lifted off your shoulders right away or at least alleviate that negative weight you've been trying to keep by yourself.

- **Celebrate Small Wins!**

We don't celebrate small accomplishments in our life as much as we should. If you have done something small that you're proud of or you accomplish a simple goal then you should make an effort to congratulate yourself or reward yourself. Do you remember when you were a child? You get rewarded every time you do something good, so do yourself a favor and catch yourself doing something good! Yes, even the small things count! You don't have to treat yourself with something big, even a simple recognition will do or a change in body language. According to research, changing your body language into powerful stances or poses or gestures can make you feel good. If you finish something, then raise your hands up as if you finish an Olympic race! It can change your mood and also raise your self – esteem.

- **Cut back the Alcohol!**

There's nothing wrong with having a good beer or occasional drinking but you drink every day because you're feeling down or whatnot it certainly won't make you feel any better. Alcohol is depressants, so if you're drinking too much then that means you're actually drinking depression itself! If you cut back this bad habit, you may actually start to find that your mood and your depressive state changes.

- **Shift to Gratitude!**

Feeling grateful is one of the greatest shifts to manage and also overcome depression. If for example you are worrying about something, and that puts you in a depressive state instead of focusing on what you don't have or focusing on those worries, think about what you have, and just be grateful for those little things because often times we take those things for granted. If you think about what you lack, it will put you into a negative mindset thus making you vulnerable to depression. When you shift into gratitude or be thankful for the things you have, it's going to put your mind into a positive mindset.

- **Take Responsibility**

You have to know that you're in control! Remember that depression is a mind game, don't let your "dark side" control you because after all YOU control both! This may be a shock to some but being depress is not just a medical condition, it's also giving in to that dark side of your mind, you somehow put yourself in this position, you let internal and external factors get the best of you – but the good news is that you are in complete control to get yourself out of it. Changing your mood is entirely up to you, take responsibility for the depressive situation you're in, and also take responsibility in knowing that you are the only person who can get yourself out of whatever situation you're in.

- **Feed the "Good Wolf," Do a Good Deed!**

Our mind as I've mentioned earlier has two sides – the good and bad. In other stories, they call it as the good wolf and the bad wolf which also applies in attitude or character. The logic is simple, whichever wolf you feed, then that's the wolf that will grow. If you do bad things, you're feeding that bad wolf in your heart and mind, on the other hand, if you do something good for others or you simply live up to your good character then you are feeding the "good wolf" and you're encouraging yourself to be a much better person.

If you're feeling down or depress, why not go do something good for someone else? It could be as simple as greeting the person next to you, or offering help to an elderly or perhaps donating something to a charity. It will not only make you feel good, it will also create another pathway in your brain that signals something positive. If you focus on yourself and your depressive situation then you are just digging a deeper hole but if you look out and try to help someone and forget about yourself for a moment it's going to put you into a positive mindset.

- **Laugh Your Heart Out!**

There's a saying that "laughter is the best medicine." Well, it certainly does apply to people who are in such a sad and depressive state. The key to not being depress all the time or not triggering those factors is to not take things seriously. Don't make a big deal out of everything. Personally, whenever I'm feeling down or sad, I acknowledge those sad feelings, probably reflect on them but not stay in that mood for too long because I know it's not going to make me feel any better. So what I do is, after acknowledging those negative feelings, I try to trigger the positive side by simply watching funny videos or comedy shows or talking to friends and family about funny stories. Laughing more, smiling more is actually an infectious disease.

Laughter will not just make you feel good, it will also make others feel good, and when you see other people enjoying your company, it will make you feel even better! Just enjoy life, tap into your inner joy and just go and have fun with the people you love or the things you wanted to do.

- **Tidy Up!**

Believe it or not, being unorganized can actually trigger depression because it's going to make your mind feel that everything is a mess. Now I'm not saying that all unorganized people are prone to being depress but it is perhaps a reflection of how their mind works. It's pretty much going to put you in a negative mindset even if you think being unorganized works out for you. Try to be more organize so that you can motivate your mindset to be more productive.

Avoiding a Relapse Depression

Relapse Depression occurs when external factors or triggers come into play, stress is perhaps the major cause of it. Stress not only worsens depression but it can actually trigger a depressive episode. Stress can come from many things like health related issues, financial problems, relationship problems like a breakup or divorce, and failing to achieve something a person always wanted. When stress comes, it's really important that you have coping tools, otherwise, stress will push you into a depressive episode or if you have just recovered from depression it can make you go back to that state again which is why it is called a relapse.

Now, we all know that stress is a part of life – and most of the time people regard it as something bad but in reality it's actually neutral. It's usually how people handle or react to it that makes it good or bad. When it comes to people diagnosed with depression, the most important thing is how they deal with stress because it can surely make and break them. If you're having trouble handling on-going stress or somebody you know is having a difficult time with it, it can lead to another depressive episode or probably the return of depressive symptoms, which if not taken care of, can ultimately worsen and create a relapse.

Most psychologists recommend that before stress comes or when you sort of notice that a situation is something of a triggering factor and can turn your mood in a downward spiral you should have three or four coping strategies that is written down so you can apply it the moment you need these strategies.

Here are some examples of stress coping strategies to avoid relapse depression:

- **Make sure that your exercise schedule has not lapsed** – if it does then try your best to get back to your exercise routine as soon as possible
- **Make sure that your diet is in check, and that your sleeping cycle is normal** – try to arrange it so that you sleep at a certain time and only eat nutritious food.
- **Talk to your therapist** – make an appointment whenever you undergo very stressful situations so that your therapist can help you assess the situation, process your feelings and help you get back on track. This is critical for you or your loved one, so if you have any significant stressors such as financial or relationship problems, work and health challenges or any kind of struggle make sure you discuss it to a medical professional.

- **Nurture Yourself -** Make sure to give yourself a breather! Treat yourself, go to a spa, relax on the beach, do that thing you love or spend time with your friends and loved ones.

If you respond to stress using these kinds of coping strategies, you won't be caught off guard or become a victim of these stressful happenings in your life. Remember that these stressful events will occur whether you like it or not, it always has and always will be, the key is how you manage it!

What Not to Do When You Are Depress

Part of managing your depression or that of your loved one is to know the things that could actually worsen the condition. In this section, we'll give you some tips on what not to do when you are undergoing depression or if you notice you are being triggered by a depressive episode.

- **Self – Medication is a No – No! -** Whenever a person is feeling down or in such a low – state, what most people do is take antidepressants. Now, if your doctor prescribed this medicine or let you drink a certain dosage whenever you're feeling depress, it's totally fine. But if you haven't gone to a medical professional and you just assumed that these drugs can make you feel better, you could actually make it worse. Depress people like stimulants but these drugs are only temporary. If a person constantly takes depressants or does self – medication without a doctor's prescription there'll be a tendency to be drug or alcohol dependent because the brain will eventually adapt to it, the problem with these drugs is that its effect is only fleeting.

- **Don't Be Isolated** – Unfortunately, this is what many depress people do – they don't pick up the phone, don't want to talk to anyone and pretty much just hide themselves away from the world. The problem with isolation is that it violates the basic law of healing from depression. You cannot be healed in isolation because humans are sort of like pack animals. We need to communicate our thoughts and feelings to other human beings otherwise we will go crazy and being in isolation will just triple the effect. Connection is what will heal a depress person, having a support system is essential to recovery.

- **Big Decisions Should Not Be Done!** - According to most psychologists, depression blocks one's intuition, and since depression is a mental problem, a person's ability to decide properly will be affected because it hinders the decision making process. So don't buy or sell your house just yet, don't get married or divorce, don't resign from your job or jump into something you're not sure of. Wait until all the depressive symptoms clear out, take the time to heal your mind so you can think straight and see things more objectively.

- **Don't Deprive Yourself** - Even if depression is a battle within your mind and emotions, you have to ensure that your body is getting the right amount of nutrients, exercise and all its physical needs so that it can function properly and help you boost your internal being. A weak body will make you feel even weaker inside, and will make you feel hopeless at a higher rate! However, you have to make sure that when it comes to eating, you only eat the right food and the proper ratio because most times whenever people feel depress, they turn to unhealthy foods (junk foods, sweets, ice creams etc.) but the problem with that is it can cause health problems like compulsive or binge eating, obesity and other illnesses.

- **Avoid asking the question of "When Will This End?"** – Here's the thing, that question will surely make you end up feeling more depress and disappointed because no one knows when! That's a wrong question to ponder on because it will only left you with despair and unwillingness to live if you're expecting that your suffering will end at a certain point and then it doesn't. Don't also ask the question "when will my depression end?" Again, nobody knows, and since your mind is not working well, you'll only tell yourself that this won't end. The best thing to do whenever you feel like asking such questions is to not focus on the future but simply focus on living in the present moment. Live one day at a time, don't think too much about what's going to happen, and focus only on something that you can control or manage, like the next 24 hours!

Chapter Five: Holistic Treatments and Therapeutic Modalities

In this chapter, we will provide you with some of the holistic forms of treatment including many therapeutic modalities that may help people who are diagnosed with any form of depression. You will also find some unconventional recommendations that could aid in alleviating depression or the depressive symptoms. Just be reminded that no alternative treatments should be considered as a replacement for professional medical advice, and forms of treatment or diet must always be taken after proper consultation, examination, diagnosis and medical prescription by a licensed professional.

It is also recommended that any alternative or complementary therapies must only be done with the approval of your psychologist or physician to make sure that all possible treatments will not have a negative effect on the brain.

Switch to Nutritious Food and the Right Diet

Switch to Paleo Diet

If you want to naturally treat your depression or recover faster, you may want to return to nature. Many holistic doctors recommend of having a more paleo – type of diet. A paleo – type of diet means that you should be eating a food that your ancestors will recognize. If you think about it, our ancestors didn't eat hamburgers, fries, sodas, or other sweet/junk foods because the body doesn't recognized those foods (and there's no Coke or McDonald's at the time yet!) because they are not considered as food but rather "food – like."

What people eat back then is only something that grows from the ground which means you should be eating something either homegrown or organic because pesticides rupture the lining of your tummy's duct wall where all the immunity is located including the serotonin receptors, which are happy neuron transmitters that control one's mood. So if you're feeding your body "trash or junk," you're going to feel like trash. You have to feed your body a good amount of nourishment that comes from earth and not "man – made" to show your body that you love it.

Some examples include legumes, lentils, veggies, fruits. If you need carbs then go natural, you can try eating brown rice or quinoa. If you are eating meat then make sure that you're looking at the sources of where this meat is coming from, know the farm, and make sure that they don't have antibiotics, pesticides or other growth hormones.

However, if you already have a good diet but may still be suffering from depressive symptoms, what you can do is to find your local holistic doctor to do a lab work to make sure that you're not missing out any antioxidants. An example is magnesium; it is a common nutrient in the nervous system with over 300 reactions in the body, so if you are lacking in magnesium, you could easily feel nervous, anxious and may have trouble in sleeping or experience constipation. So if you're just lacking in one nutrient it can surely affect your functioning – what you eat is really important.

Avoid Diet Sweeteners

Sweeteners can cause depressive symptoms or even bipolar disorder because some of it acts as excito - toxins in your neurons which can result to imbalance in your brain that can end up in having depression or other mental disorders. Never take diet sweeteners such as raw honey, natural maple syrup, sweeteners with fruit or coconut palm sugars.

Healthy Fats

Eating healthy fats is another alternative in treating depression. Healthy fats include omega – 3 fatty acids, some kind of organic butter, coconut oil, avocado, and the likes. These examples can ultimately heal the brain. Our brain is actually composed of 60% fat; eating wrong kind of fats can make your brain cells as well as neurotransmitter not properly function, and may again cause an imbalance which can lead to depression.

Heal Your Digestion

Your stomach and digestion has its own system with over a hundred million neurons that helps in activating many neurotransmitters. An example is your digestive intestines; your intestines is in charge of serotonin production, so instead of taking a serotonin inhibitor to add this chemical in your neurons; you can have a healthy tummy or a healthy digestive system that produces more serotonin that will eventually get to your brain. Of course, don't go off your medications or antidepressants without your doctor's approval but just take into consideration that if your digestion is healthy, it's a great way to use up the serotonin production in your body that will heal your brain.

Holistic Supplements

Natural Neuro – Transmitters

Holistic supplements can also fix mood disorders especially among depress patients. Natural neurotransmitters such as GABA, L theanine, 5HDP can work wonders for some people especially for those who have trouble sleeping.

Homeopathy Herbs

Herbs like kava - kava roots, lavender, Goldcap flower, the list is endless about herbs that are homegrown or organic that can be used to treat depressive moods.

B - Vitamins

B – Vitamins are also important if you are looking for an alternative treatment but it is often overlooked. B – Vitamins are definitely needed in the body because it aids in detoxification and methylation.

Other Modalities

An example of this treatment is something that could particularly help post – traumatic patients as well as people who have severe anxiety disorders.

Bio – Neuro Feedback

Bio – neuro feedback is a non – evasive procedure that really works. The process involves putting electrodes on your brain, and then they do a brain map. After which doctors are then able to diagnose a patient based on the brain map and brain waves. The remedy is simply watching a movie of your choice, the sound and picture goes in and out and as a result the brain sort of freaks out or gets confused and then it will eventually adjust. This is good because it forms new neural connection and pathways that helps in decreasing anxiety and mood disorders over time and can also increase the quality of sleep.

Alpha - Stim

There's a device that will be connected to your ear which will measure and regulate your brain waves, and then immediately takes away the anxiety. This type of method is actually being used in a lot of hospitals nowadays.

Mind and Body Therapies

Mindful practices like meditation, yoga, qigong can put you in the moment, and anyone who is depressed is projecting their consciousness in the past which is why these patients are quite regretful. Only the present moment is what we have and mindful practices like this keep us in the "now."

Techniques for Healing Emotional Trauma

The most common technique to heal past traumas is through visualization, radiant tapping as well as a method called cellular release therapy. You can either enroll on a motivational class that do these techniques, get a mental coach perhaps, attend seminars or even watch or listen on meditative techniques online. You can also talk to your psychiatrist about it so that he/she can recommend you to a motivational guru or psych mentor of some sort.

Reduce Stress through Mindful Techniques

When there's too much stress in life, many people gets overwhelmed and may feel as if the whole world crashed into them, this stresses can ultimately triple the effect of depressive symptoms. This is why mindful therapies such as meditation, yoga, tai - chi and the likes can be of great help in reducing stress.

Meditation is effective because it has been proven to inhibit the signals to and from the brain's amygdala. Amygdala causes stress, fear and aggression, which is why meditation works best because it activates the part of your brain that is in charge of feelings of love, connection, safety and security.

Deep Belly Breathing

Deep belly breathing works when you constrict the back of your throat so that when you inhale your breath is long, slow and deep, this is also how baby's actually breathe wherein when they inhale they push their bellies out as compared to depress patients where most of the time only do shallow breathings. This could be of help in naturally treating depression.

Move, move, move!

One of the best ways in treating depression naturally is to make sure that you physically move! When depress patients are always thinking too much, the tendency is to implode from all the thinking, fears, worries and stresses which of course will lead to worsening the condition. This is why you need to move! Be in your body, get out of the house, be under the sun, go take a walk, exercise, swim, play some sports and just get physical! When you are moving, you're body produces endorphins or the "feel – good hormones" that can help increase your happiness and reduce depression. As much as possible, you need to connect with nature or be in nature because it's actually soothing for your overall being.

According to scientists, nature has its own type of healing vibration called the Schumann Resonance. This is when the earth vibrates at around 7 cycles per second which is what your brain vibrates at in its alpha state. This can make your mind heal and be in a productive and focused state so spend as much time in nature as you can.

Set a Vision or Purpose for Your Life

Sometimes the sense of worthlessness or hopelessness is the root cause or main reason why a lot of people become a victim of depression. If you think that you're not doing what you're supposed to be doing or you're not living the life you always wanted or you're not achieving your dreams that could all contribute to having depression or stress, and that feeling of being "worthless." Again, you can use visualization techniques, meditation as well as affirmations to help improve your inner state.

What most people do to maximize the power of these techniques is to imagine or see yourself living the life, having those things, being in that ideal relationship or simply dreaming of something big, which you can do every morning or before you go to sleep. Just feel it on a vibration level or in the cells of your body so you can start creating a shift in your mind and focus towards success in those areas so that you can create a positive momentum in your life.

Neuro – Emotional Training

This technique is also known as applied kinesiology or muscle testing. Hidden or past emotions like pain and trauma can be hidden in our organs and even on our body's tissues but most of the time we don't know it because the body has an innate intelligence that we consciously are not aware of. There's a disconnection in the subconscious mind and our consciousness which is why neuro – emotional technique can come in handy.

What this method does is it enables the body to test concept and remember it, once the body remembers something that has happened and there's a trauma that it's holding, the patient will be able to clear it or let go of it with a conscious mind. The key is to having the subconscious mind connect to the conscious mind to be able to clear the traumatic experience that the body is holding.

Chapter Six: How to Help a Depress Person

Dealing with someone who is depressed is not an easy thing especially if that someone is a loved one, a family member or a close friend. Most of the time, we try to help are loved ones fight depression and we want to support them all the way but sometimes it's not very helpful. In this chapter, you'll learn some tips on how to deal with someone who is depress; how you can help them, what's your role as a supporter, and how to say things to them that could encourage them to get better. We will also make you understand the reason behind why they act this way.

Tips in Dealing with a Depress Person

Tip #1: Your Presence is a Must!

The number one thing that you need to do for somebody that is currently dealing with depression whether it's a friend or family member is to simply be there for them as much as possible. Of course, if they are an introvert you're going to need to give them a little bit of space. But by being present with them, they'll know and feel that you genuinely care as a human being. Many people who were diagnosed and who overcame depression can attest that this method is perhaps the best way to help a loved one to cope up with depressive moods; it will surely go a long way at helping people through their treatment or current condition.

Tip #2: Encourage them to Socialize

Encourage them to get out socially with you. Just get them out of the house! Of course, they're going to resist it, and you'll probably end up fighting with them but try and push them anyway because they know deep inside that if they get out of the house, they will start to feel better because they will get to see things, their surroundings will change, they'll probably interact with some people (even if they don't want to). The bottom line is that going out will take their minds off their own mind! If you continue to check in on them from time to time, and you show an interest then they'll know that you care even if they don't appear to not care at all.

Tip #3: Encourage them to Set Goals!

Another thing you could do to help is to maybe push them to set goals on what they want and help them to find a reason that they want to get better from depression. If you try to just lead them towards treatment whether seeking medical help from a psychiatrist, counselors or other health professionals (which is of course, highly encourage) but it's something that you want not because they want it, they might go to therapy and do it for a short period of time or only put in a little effort but chances are they're not really going to embody what it means to get better. So why not create what people call a "structural tension"? Help them find an activity or something in their life that they want to do or something that they are interested in (even if at this point, they may not be really interested in anything).

This will be a difficult thing to do but if you as a family member, a friend or someone who just truly care for them, if you could just help them take one step at a time, little by little, and stay patient it will surely go a long way and it will help them recover faster.

Tip #4: Encourage them to focus on positivity!

If you are someone who hasn't dealt with any type of depression yourself, then for sure you'll never experience that deep sadness or you may have never felt that kind of negativity. What you can do is to help them remember and focus on the good things on their life or the happy memories you have shared with them because they need that positive energy. Depress people are usually in a place where they can't generate positivity or even a bit of genuine happiness on their own at this situation, so help them out with that! Get them to laugh, tell jokes, show funny videos, do something fun together, just do anything you can to help cheer them up or boost their downtrodden souls even if it seems impossible at the moment.

Tip #5: Be an Advocate and a Supporter!

The last thing you can do that will surely help them recover is by being an advocate for them when it comes to seeking treatment. A lot of depress people don't really like seeking help from others but if you do have a good relationship with them, you can try to encourage them to do so because sometimes even if they're ready they choose not to seek treatment themselves because there's a social stigma when it comes to mental health disorders. They might feel embarrassed or they might think they're crazy for doing so. But who knows? You might be the person who can help them go along the road of getting better.

Tip #6: Say the Right Things

There are things that we need to know about what's helpful and what might not be. The first one is saying things that we think are helpful but actually aren't.

Avoid the following phrases or something similar:

- "You just need to get out of the house"
- "You just need to look on the bright side"
- "You got to think positive"
- "Just go get some fresh air, you'll be fine"

- "Don't mind it, everyone gets depress!"
- "You'll get over it like everyone does"
- "We all have bad days, just don't focus on it"

Saying stuff like that to someone who is depressed doesn't actually help them feel better because depression is not just a matter of having a bad day or feeling sad. Remember that depression is a mental illness; it's not something that a person can help or easily get over. If you say things like that it can often times make them feel even more helpless because they just can't get over it.

Instead of saying those things, here is what you should say to someone who is depressed that are helpful:

- "I believe in you"
- "I love you"
- "I care for you"
- "I'm here to support you"
- "You are strong and I think you can get through this"…or something like "I can help you get through this"

Just be honest when saying those kinds of words of encouragement.

Tip #7: Don't Ever Offer Advice to Someone Who is Depress!

This is actually not just for people who are depress or who has mental disorders, this is for people in general because sometimes we don't want to get advice especially from people who aren't experts at that particular thing.

Avoid giving advices like the following:

- "You should exercise more"
- "You need to see a doctor/therapist"
- "You need to eat nutritious foods"
- "You should do this or do that"
- "Keep moving, get up!"

Giving these kinds of advices is actually helpful because it can really help in treating depression just like what we previously discuss in the past chapters. However, if you tell a depress person things like these and give advice on what they should and shouldn't do, it can most likely make them feel bad. I mean, generally, myself included, we don't want to be told what to do or what not to do even if sometimes it's the right thing to do, it just feels like we're not in control or we just need to follow certain orders even if it comes from a good place. For people who are depress, it's the same thing, it could make them helpless and feel frustrated.

You can still give words of advice to your depressed loved one or friend but instead of saying "you should do this or that" you can change your approach and say things like:

- "What kind of things have you found out or learned about that can help with your depression and have you tried doing that?"
- "I've heard about or I've learned about some solutions for people with depression, are you interested in knowing some tips?"

If they say no, it's fine don't push the idea to them or don't force them to listen to you (otherwise you're still telling them what to do) but if ever they do say yes, then that's the time you can share your ideas or some suggestions that could be helpful in treating their conditions.

Tip #8: Understand that your loved one or friend may pull away from you because they don't want to burden you with their depression

Sometimes depress people tend to push their loved ones or friends away, and you have to understand that it's not because they don't love you or care about you, it's because they are feeling overwhelmed and they don't want to overwhelm you or put the burden on you. Most of the times, these people feel awful and they don't want to make you feel or their loved ones feel that same depress feeling which is why they will pull back.

So it's okay if they're not answering your phone calls, not seeing you or anyone, not in the mood to talk to you or what not, though of course you should still check on them from time to time but try to understand that they need some space. What you can do is to just remind them that you love them, you care for them, and that you're there for them whenever they're ready to talk. You have to also keep in mind that even if they're pulling back or you're sort of giving them space you should still keep on communicating with them at least in a subtle way or not be so 'pushy' because this is the time when their brain/depression tells them that no one cares for them or whatnot. Keep affirming them and just support them.

Tip #9: Don't make ultimatums

Never make ultimatums or give 'tough' love or say things like "if you don't get better or stop being depress, I'm going to leave you or break up with you" or whatnot because these things are not just destructive but can also worsen their current condition. It will make them feel more depress and trap. Don't ever tell them your feelings directly or make them feel threatened so that they will be force to get well or change because that's not going to work and for some it could be dangerous for them because they could be suicidal.

Tip#11: Be a listener

If someone is talking to you about their depression or what they're going through or how they're feeling, you should make sure to just listen. Try not to compare your experience to them or make it about you. Depress people need somebody to be there for them, so if ever they open up to you make sure that you don't make a big fuss about it or tell others about it especially if they're particularly shy to tell everyone. Sometimes they just need to feel heard and valued despite of what they're going through. Listening is very important because it can literally save a life!

Tip#12: Don't forget to take care of yourself

If you have a loved one or family member who is undergoing depression, it could also be draining, upsetting and challenging which is why you should also be taking care of yourself. Don't ever think that you have to "fix" them or make them solely your responsibility (even for parents or spouses) because you just can't. You can't just solve depression right away, there's a process and it will take some time to heal from it.

So instead of making your loved one's depression a problem or something that makes you worry because you can't find a solution, be a supporter instead and not a "fixer." It'll be way less challenging and exhausting for you.

Chapter Seven: The Future of Depression

In this chapter, we will share with you the new types of treatments being done for those who are struggling with depression as well as what the future may hold for patients with other mental disorders in general. The possible technology that will create a much efficient way in diagnosing depression looks promising, the new medical approaches as well as the up and coming high – tech brain treatments to heal depression and prevent it from recurring is what scientists and researchers are currently doing to give hope to those who have been battling the disorder.

New Treatments for Depression

Deep Trans - Cranial Magnetic Stimulation (TMS)

Deep TMS uses a unique magnetic coil that focuses on the magnetic pulses so that it can go deeper than traditional or surface TMS. Deep TMS technology allows more areas of the brain to be stimulated especially the pre – frontal cortex' subsequent pathways, these pathways will be activated and can help patients suffering from depression and addiction as well as those who have OCD. The symptoms of such mental conditions are essentially alleviated.

Scientists are quite excited for the future advancements of TMS because this technology could allow in modulating the nuclei areas of the brain because such areas are responsible in addiction medicine's pathology.

A typical treatment protocol for deep TMS involves a 20 minute session that does not involve any type of fasting or even a change in the current medications being taken by the patients. Patients can normally function after being treated because it doesn't cause any sleepiness or sedation, and the patient can even drive after undergoing treatment.

Usually the patient is recommended to go through 30 sessions; the promising thing about TMS is that the patients who have tried it so far are noticing improvements in their condition just after the 2nd or 3rd week of session, although most doctors still recommend finishing the required sessions to have a continued benefit from depressive symptoms. Most patients who tried are happily reporting that they can now control their depression and perhaps prevent depressive symptoms from developing further.

How does TMS work?

The first day of the deep TMS treatment involves cortical mapping. This is a process where doctors are finding a spot on the brain called the motor cortex that is located on the left side of the brain which controls the motor functioning of the right hand. Once this spot is located, the area in the pre – frontal cortex (part of the brain that is responsible for mood regulation) is assessed to be 5 – 6 cm which can help the motor cortex area.

According to many studies, 55 % of the patients do not respond to their first trial of medication, what's more interesting is that about 30% of the patients do not respond at all to any sort of drug therapy. These patients are at a high risk for suicide as well as self – medication (which is quite dangerous given their brain's condition). This is why TMS has been developing because scientists want to treat these mental conditions and so that they can also improve the chances of patients have a "relapse – free" lifestyle.

When it comes to deep TMS, the basis of the effectiveness is the response and remission rates. Response means that when the symptoms of depression declines by about 50% following the treatment but the patients could still exhibit many symptoms that make it hard for them to maintain normal functioning in their day to day lives. Remission on the other hand is when the depressive symptoms have virtually disappear or have been gone making the patients function at the highest level of their capacity. Someone with remission can work normally without the interference of the symptoms.

TMS has over 70% response rate and over 30% remission rates, which are significantly higher than any given medication especially for those patients who are not responding to previous drugs. Between 20 and 30 sessions; the 30 sessions have a higher response rate as well as remission rates compared to 20 sessions.

Deep TMS vs. Surface TMS

The deep TMS is significantly higher who have previously had surface TMS and are having continuous difficulty with the depression or their symptoms. Deep TMS has shown better response and remission rates.

In terms of technology, scientists are finding that deep TMS has more activation areas in the brain because of the deeper penetration of the magnetic pulses. Deep TMS doesn't also use high energy level compared to surface TMS.

Aside from depression, deep TMS has been already approved to heal conditions like dementia, stroke, autism, Parkinson's disease, bipolar disorder and schizophrenia. Companies and researchers are still conducting clinical trials to look at other possible uses in treating other mental conditions like OCD, nicotine dependence and PTSD as well as various neurological and psychiatric conditions using the deep TMS.

The Future of Deep TMS

Scientists are also looking at developing magnetic coils with different configurations for various mental conditions. There will be other coils with different helmets that will be used for different neuropsychological disorders just like the H – coil which was approved by the FDA for treating depression.

The deep TMS treatment is mostly used in many academic institutions and it is also now being adapted in the U.S. Navy. There have been some interests among doctors if the treatment can also be used for PTSD patients like the veterans. For now, researchers are still focusing on how to further improve this treatment especially for patients diagnosed with severe depression and anxiety and how it can be more main stream just like ECT and surface TMS treatments.

Promising Treatments for Depression

Glutamate System Manipulation through Ketamine

Glutamate is an excitatory amino acid in the brain, and intracellular glutamate seems to play a very important role in regulation of mood, thinking, and perception. A drug that antagonizes a particular type of glutamate receptor called the NMDA Receptor has been shown to be quite promising when it comes to treating depression.

Many people especially depress patients are now becoming increasingly familiar with the drug called Ketamine. It's an anesthetic that has been around for quite a long time, and that's been somewhat proven in recent years to have a value in terms of treating depression very quickly; the delivery of its rapid and robust response to depression that has been effective within just 1 hour or two of it being infused in the patient. Studies have shown that about 1/3 of patients who received an intravenous ketamine infusion hold on to their response in just about a week.

Ketamine, in many ways, is one of the most promising new solutions for treating depression but according to scientists and doctors, it still might not be quite ready yet because even if it is a very valuable drug where it can potentially have an antidepressant and psychotic effect as well as anesthetic effect it still needs to be carefully monitored. It's not yet set up for outpatient practices or to become somewhat "main stream," and there are still many unanswered questions like how does a patient sustain a response to ketamine? It could be like ECT that can have an effect to patients when it comes to preventing relapse or remissions and other mental issues but many researchers and psychologists are making an effort to study its potential value, and its role as a preventative drug. Scientists are also looking at the effects of multiple dose administrations or other possible medicines that could sustain a response.

Magnetic Seizure Therapy (MST)

MST is a focally and magnetic induced seizure. It is focal in a way that it doesn't spread throughout the brain that could cause widespread activation. It only gets through the cortex and only targets particular neurons inside the brain. Researchers are still evaluating the early stages of MST so that they could understand how to best deliver this treatment in an effort to optimize its response and try to make it as good as ECT. Since ECT has some side effects, they're trying to make MST not have certain side effects in the brain or in the body so that there could be a better treatment for patients diagnosed with depression.

Future of Assessing Depression among Patients

EEG Techniques

Researchers are now creating a machine learning device that could extract information from very large amount of data to predict if a patient will respond to the medication. This will be based on the patient's brainwave patterns that will be recorded using EEG devices. This technique could lead to having a customized anti – depressants for patients instead of a trial and error methods being implemented by most psychologists.

Online Testing for Depression

Online tests will be used to diagnose depression by creating an algorithm or a set of codes that can predict and hopefully prevent the diagnosis of a new depressive episode.

Content Analysis Tools

In Israel, a software is being developed to identify the potential diagnosis of depression via analyzing the patient's writings because it can indicate the person's psychological state and can also serve as a screening method for depression.

MagnetoEncephaloGraphy (MEG)

MEG is currently used in measuring the activities of the brain but scientists are also finding ways on how it can be used in pinpointing the source of seizures among epilepsy patients. It can also be used to diagnose dementia, traumatic brain injuries, migraine, PTSD and depression in the future.

Speech Recognition Software

Similar to the content analysis tool that is being developed, the speech recognition software aims to detect signs of depression via the quality of the patient's voice. It aims to analyze the subtle symptoms in a person's voice like awkwardness, anxiety or being in a depressed state.

Brain Live Streaming

Many researchers are now trying to find ways on how they can watch the brain while it is live! Of course, this is still far from the future but scientists are hopeful that if there will be this kind of technology, it could detect early symptoms of depression by directly watching a person's brain activity including the emotions, thoughts, pain while it is happening all at once. Making people see how they literally feel!

Bonus Chapter:
Famous People Who Have Depression

Depression is something that we all share at some point in our lives, and though some of us may not literally be diagnose with clinical depression, we can all agree that the feeling of sadness and inner struggle is what all of us have already experienced in our lives. It could come from many things such as social and environmental stress, relationship problems and even from our own mindset. All of these things contribute to depression but it shouldn't stop us from achieving our true potential.

If you have read the history of depression or melancholia, we discuss how some past generations see this disorder in a more positive way – they see it not as a mental disease but as something that pushes the boundaries of creativity, a force that could tap the "genius" within, and something that most great inventors and artists share which enabled them to achieve great feats.

In this bonus chapter, you will get to know some of the most famous Hollywood celebrities and artists who were diagnosed with depression. They did not let depression get the best of them; they actually get the most out of depression and use it to their advantage!

Notable Hollywood Celebrities and Artists diagnosed with Depression:

1. Lady Gaga
Known For: Music albums; The Fame, Born This Way, Artpop, Cheek to Cheek, Joanne

2. Angelina Jolie
Known For: Film roles; Maleficent, Salt, Tomb Raider, The Tourist, Mr. & Mrs. Smith

3. Brad Pitt

Known For: Film roles; Ocean's Eleven Trilogy, Meet Joe Black, Troy, The Mexican, Inglorious Basterds, The Curious Case of Benjamin Button, Fight Club, Allied, Moneyball

4. Johnny Depp

Known For: Film roles; The Pirates of the Caribbean Trilogy, Edward Scissorhands, Dark Shadows, Charlie and the Chocolate Factory, Transcendance, Black Mass

5. Harrison Ford

Known For: Film roles; Star Wars: The Empire Strikes Back, Star Wars: The Return of the Jedi, Star Wars: The Force Awakens, Indiana Jones, Air Force One, 42, Cowboys & Aliens

6. Anne Hathaway

Known For: Film roles; The Princess Diaries, Love & Other Drugs, Les Miserables, The Dark Knight Rises, The Devil Wears Prada, Bride Wars, The Intern, Ella Enchanted, One Day

7. Eminem

Known For: Music albums; Infinite, The Slim Shady, The Marshall Mathers LP, Relapse, Recovery, The Marshall Mathers LP 2,

8. Jim Carrey

Known For: Film roles; Dumb and Dumber, The Mask, The Truman Show, Ace Ventura: Pet Detective, Bruce Almighty, Liar, Liar, A Series of Unfortunate Events, A Christmas Carol

9. Matthew Perry

Known For: TV & Film roles; Friends, Mr. Sunshine, Odd Couple, 17 Again, Birds of America, Numb

10. J.K. Rowling

Known For: Best – Selling Author & Executive Producer; Harry Potter books and movie franchise, Fantastic Beast & Where to Find Them

11. Ellen DeGeneres

Known For: Voice actor & talk show host; Ellen, Finding Nemo, Finding Dory, American Idol

12. Britney Spears

Known For: Music albums; Baby One More Time, Oops!...I Did It Again, In the Zone, Greatest Hits: My Prerogative

13. Dwayne "The Rock" Johnson

Known For: Wrestler & Film roles; WWE, San Andreas, Moana, Hercules, Fast & Furious franchise, G.I. Joe Retaliation, Get Smart, Central Intelligence, Tooth Fairy

14. Jon Hamm

Known For: TV & Film roles; Mad Men, Baby Driver, Minions, Million Dollar Arm, We Were Soldiers, Shrek, Keeping Up with the Jonesses, The Town

15. Sarah Silverman

Known For: Comedian & film roles; Saturday Night Live, Wreck – It Ralph, The Sarah Silverman Program, Sarah Silverman: A Speck of Dust (Netflix comedy special)

16. Catherine Zeta Jones

Known For: Film roles; Ocean's Twelve, No Reservations, The Legend of Zorro, Rock of Ages, The Rebound, Red 2

17. Owen Wilson

Known For: Film roles; Zoolander, Wedding Crashers, No Escape, Marley & Me, The Internship, Hall Pass, Shanghai Noon, Cars

18. Trever Noah
Known For: Comedian & talk show host; The Daily Show with Trevor Noah, The Amazing Date, Tonight with Trevor Noah

19. Conan O'Brien
Known For: Comedian & talk show host; Late Night with Conan O'Brien, The Tonight Show with Conan O'Brien, Conan, Saturday Night Live

20. Robin Williams
Known For: Film roles; Dead Poets Society, Good Will Hunting, Mrs. Doubtfire, Night at the Museum, Bicentennial Man, RV, Jumanji, Man of the Year, License to Wed, Hook

Index

A

acupuncture	88
akinesis/bradykinesia	67
alien hand syndrome	67
alternative treatments	88, 90
antidepressants	45
antigoagulants	45
antihypertensives	45
Apathy/Inertia	3, 60
Apraxia	3, 67
aromatherapy	88
ayurvedic medicine	88

B

behavioral and mood changes	30
biofeedback techniques	88
brain scans	42, 53
bright light therapy	88

C

Caregiver	4
CBD	65
changes in vision	29
CJD	71
Clinical Studies	95
Cognitive and mental stimulation exercises	55, 90
cognitive deterioration	58
Communication and language	9
compulsive behaviors	57

confusion	29, 30, 31
cutting down on alcohol	45

D

delusions	4, 30, 34, 40, 55, 57, 78
depression	4, 9, 22, 29, 34, 39, 50, 59, 61, 69, 72, 78, 80, 84, 85
Diagnosis	1, 4, 5, 32, 42, 52, 53, 59, 133
difficulties in problem solving or decision-making	39
Disinhibition	60, 61
disturbances of motor functions	56

E

eating healthy	46, 90
Executive Function	5
Exercise	95
extreme behavior and mood changes	31

F

Functional Impairment	5

H

Hallucination	5, 31
herbal medicine	88
history	13
homeopathy	88

I

Imaging	95

Incontinence   5
Infections   80
International Efforts   6, 96
irritability and anxiety   78

L

language difficulties   39
Lifestyle Changes   6, 45, 90
Losing weight   45, 90

M

massage   88
Meditation   90
mental stimulation or cognitive therapies   74
mood changes   39
muffled speech   78

N

Neurons   5

O

obesity   32

P

physical exercise   74
physical mobility and coordination   31
poor diet   32
prominent or dramatic behavioral changes   57

R

Reduce or quit drinking alcohol   90
regular exercise   46
Relaxation techniques and exercises   90
Research   1, 6, 93, 94, 95, 122
restlessness and agitation   39

S

Signs and Symptoms   4, 5, 28, 38, 49, 56, 118
Sleep studies   96
sleep disturbances   30, 78
smoking   32, 33, 45, 52, 90
Stem cell research   96
stress management   90
sudden mood changes   30
supportive treatments   54

T

Treatment Options   4, 5, 33, 44, 54, 61
trouble with daily tasks   29

V

vitamin and mineral supplements   9

Photo References

Page 8 Photo by user tumisu via Pixabay.com, https://pixabay.com/en/mental-health-brain-thinking-2313430/

Page 12 Photo by user Sander van der Wel via Flickr.com, https://www.flickr.com/photos/jar0d/4649749639/

Page 28 Photo by user Anemone123 via Pixabay.com, https://pixabay.com/en/desperate-sad-depressed-feet-hands-2293377/

Page 36 Photo by user Drew Leavy via Flickr.com, https://www.flickr.com/photos/drewleavy/4638947724/

Page 61 Photo by user Free – Photos via Pixabay.com, https://pixabay.com/en/window-view-sitting-indoors-girl-1081788/

Page 78 Photo by user Sebastien Wiertz via Flickr.com, https://www.flickr.com/photos/wiertz/6093566215/

Page 89 Photo by user Anemone via Pixabay.com,

https://pixabay.com/en/girlfriends-hug-trust-girl-2213259/

Page 101 Photo by user aytuguluturk via Pixabay.com, https://pixabay.com/en/mechanical-brain-man-machine-2033446/

Page 112 Photo by user Ver en vivo En Directo via Flickr.com, https://www.flickr.com/photos/39844802@N08/16434210740/

References

"5 Key Elements of Recovery from Depression and Substance Abuse" Promises.com

https://www.promises.com/articles/addiction-recovery/5-key-elements-of-recovery/

"9 Depression Types to Know" Everyday Health

https://www.everydayhealth.com/depression-pictures/different-types-of-depression.aspx

"10 Depression Myths We Need To Stop Believing" Huffington Post

http://www.huffingtonpost.com/2014/09/03/depression-myths_n_5715453.html

"10 Ways to Cope With Depression" Everyday Health

https://www.everydayhealth.com/depression-photos/ways-to-cope-with-depression.aspx

"20 Celebrities Who Battled Depression" Health.com

http://www.health.com/health/gallery/0,,20526304,00.html

"30 Famous People Alive Today Who Have Battled Depression" SocialWorkDegreeGuide.com

http://www.socialworkdegreeguide.com/30-famous-people-alive-today-battled-depression/

"Adolescent Health and Youths of Color" National Association of Social Workers

http://www.naswdc.org/practice/adolescent_health/ah0203.asp

"Causes of Depression" Depressionhurts.ca

http://depressionhurts.ca/en/about/causes.aspx

"Causes of Depression" WebMd.com

http://www.webmd.com/depression/guide/causes-depression#1

"Depression" MedlinePlus.gov

https://medlineplus.gov/depression.html

"Depression: 7 Powerful Tips to Help You Overcome Bad Moods" PsychologyToday.com https://www.psychologytoday.com/blog/anxiety-zen/201605/depression-7-powerful-tips-help-you-overcome-bad-moods

"Depression Diagnosis" Webmd.com

http://www.webmd.com/depression/guide/depression-diagnosis#1

"Depression Damages Parts of the Brain, Research Concludes" The Conversation

http://theconversation.com/depression-damages-parts-of-the-brain-research-concludes-43915

"Depression Differential Diagnoses" Medscape.com

http://emedicine.medscape.com/article/286759-differential

"Depression: Do You Know the Symptoms?" Webmd.com

http://www.webmd.com/depression/default.htm

"Depression myths and fact" MedBroadcast.com

http://www.medbroadcast.com/channel/mental-health/depression/depression-myths-and-fact

"Depression Relapse: What Can Trigger It and How to Prevent It" US News

http://health.usnews.com/health-care/patient-advice/articles/2017-06-13/depression-relapse-what-can-trigger-it-and-how-to-prevent-it

"Diagnosis of depression" HealthDirect.com

https://www.healthdirect.gov.au/diagnosis-of-depression

"Herbs and Supplements for Depression"Healthline.com

http://www.healthline.com/health/depression/herbs-supplements

"How Depression Affects Your Brain Structure" Collective Evolution

http://www.collective-evolution.com/2016/02/19/how-depression-affects-brain-structure-what-you-can-do-to-change-it-back/

"How to help a friend with depression" Reachout.com

https://au.reachout.com/articles/how-to-help-a-friend-with-depression

"Hope For Depression: Recent Innovation and Future Prospects" MentalHealthRoundTable.ca

http://www.mentalhealthroundtable.ca/report/Hope_for_Depression.pdf

"Leashing the Black Dog: The History of Depression" Art of Manliness

http://www.artofmanliness.com/2015/03/16/the-history-of-depression/

"Magnetic Seizure Therapy Promising for Major Depression" Medscape.com

http://www.medscape.com/viewarticle/773812

"Natural Depression Treatment" DrWeil.com

https://www.drweil.com/health-wellness/body-mind-spirit/mental-health/natural-depression-treatment/

"Phases of clinical depression could affect treatment" University of Adelaide

https://www.adelaide.edu.au/news/news72122.html

"Signs and symptoms" BeyondBlue.org

https://www.beyondblue.org.au/the-facts/depression/signs-and-symptoms

"The Best Natural Treatments for Depression" Everyday Health

https://www.everydayhealth.com/depression/treating/alternative-treatments.aspx

"The Stages of Depression Treatment" HealthGrades.com

https://healthguides.healthgrades.com/finding-the-best-depression-treatment/the-stages-of-depression-treatment

"Top 10 Signs of Depression" PsychCentral.com

https://psychcentral.com/lib/top-10-signs-of-depression/

"Types of Depression" Webmd.com

http://www.webmd.com/depression/guide/depression-types#1

"Warning Signs & Types of Depression" Psychcentral.com

https://psychcentral.com/lib/types-and-symptoms-of-depression/

"What causes depression?" Comh.ca

http://www.comh.ca/antidepressant-skills/work/workbook/pages/section1-04.cfm

"What Is Depression?" American Psychiatric Association

https://www.psychiatry.org/patients-families/depression/what-is-depression

Feeding Baby
Cynthia Cherry
978-1941070000

Axolotl
Lolly Brown
978-0989658430

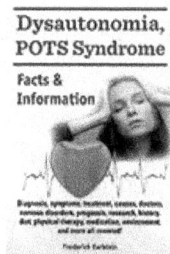

Dysautonomia, POTS
Syndrome
Frederick Earlstein
978-0989658485

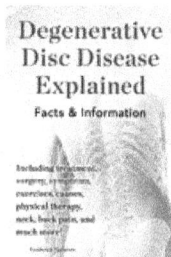

Degenerative Disc
Disease Explained
Frederick Earlstein
978-0989658485

Sinusitis, Hay Fever,
Allergic Rhinitis Explained
Frederick Earlstein
978-1941070024

Wicca
Riley Star
978-1941070130

Zombie Apocalypse
Rex Cutty
978-1941070154

Capybara
Lolly Brown
978-1941070062

Eels As Pets
Lolly Brown
978-1941070167

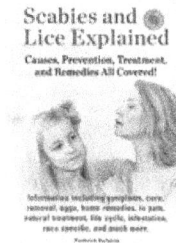

Scabies and Lice Explained
Frederick Earlstein
978-1941070017

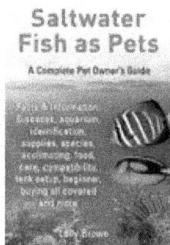

Saltwater Fish As Pets
Lolly Brown
978-0989658461

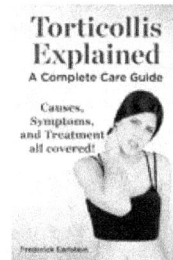

Torticollis Explained
Frederick Earlstein
978-1941070055

Kennel Cough
Lolly Brown
978-0989658409

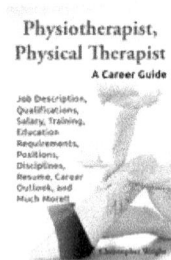

Physiotherapist, Physical
Therapist
Christopher Wright
978-0989658492

Rats, Mice, and Dormice
As Pets
Lolly Brown
978-1941070079

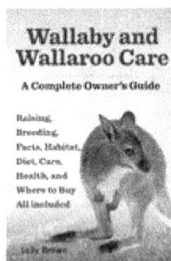

Wallaby and Wallaroo Care
Lolly Brown
978-1941070031

Bodybuilding Supplements
Explained
Jon Shelton
978-1941070239

Demonology
Riley Star
978-19401070314

Pigeon Racing
Lolly Brown
978-1941070307

Dwarf Hamster
Lolly Brown
978-1941070390

Cryptozoology
Rex Cutty
978-1941070406

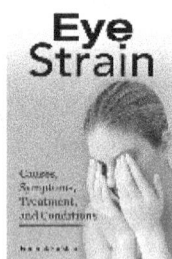

Eye Strain
Frederick Earlstein
978-1941070369

Inez The Miniature Elephant
Asher Ray
978-1941070353

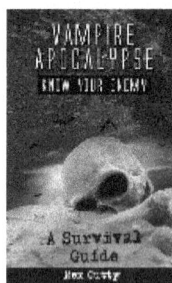

Vampire Apocalypse
Rex Cutty
978-1941070321

www.ingramcontent.com/pod-product-compliance
Lightning Source LLC
Chambersburg PA
CBHW060908280326
41934CB00007B/1238